To my children, Jason, Peter, and Caroline,
and to children everywhere—
you have been my inspiration all along
—VK

To my mom, Terri, who has been there
every step of the way with me, and
to my grandma, Cornelia, who was the
spitting image of Ella Fitzgerald
—AH

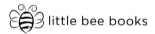 little bee books

251 Park Avenue South, New York, NY 10010
Text copyright © 2020 by Vivian Kirkfield
Illustrations copyright © 2020 by Alleanna Harris
Photo (page 35) copyright © by Getty/Bettmann
First Edition | Manufactured in China TPL 0120
2 4 6 8 10 9 7 5 3 1
Library of Congress Cataloging-in-Publication Data
Names: Kirkfield, Vivian, author. | Harris, Alleanna, illustrator.
Title: Making their voices heard: the inspiring friendship of Ella
Fitzgerald and Marilyn Monroe / by Vivian Kirkfield; illustrated by Alleanna Harris.
Description: First edition. | New York, NY: Little Bee Books, [2020] | Audience: Grades K–3.
Identifiers: LCCN 2019018001 | Subjects: LCSH: Fitzgerald, Ella—Juvenile literature.
Monroe, Marilyn, 1926–1962—Juvenile literature.
Jazz musicians—United States—Biography—Juvenile literature.
Singers—United States—Biography—Juvenile literature. |
Motion picture actors and Actresses—United States—Biography—Juvenile literature.
Classification: LCC ML3930.F5 K57 2020 | DDC 782.42165092 [B]—dc23
LC record available at https://lccn.loc.gov/2019018001
ISBN 978-1-4998-0915-2
littlebeebooks.com

For more information about special discounts on bulk purchases,
please contact Little Bee Books at sales@littlebeebooks.com.

MAKING THEIR VOICES HEARD

• The Inspiring Friendship of Ella Fitzgerald and Marilyn Monroe •

Words by
VIVIAN KIRKFIELD

Art by
ALLEANNA HARRIS

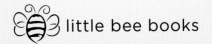 little bee books

Ella and Marilyn.

On the outside, you couldn't find two girls who looked more different.
But on the inside, they were alike—full of hopes and dreams,
and plans of what might be.

Ella sang for her supper on the streets of New York City, but she
dreamed of sharing her voice with the world. When she stepped
onstage for an Amateur Night competition at the Apollo Theater,
her voice brought the crowd to their feet.

Goodbye, street life.

Hello, jazz band!

Song after song, Ella scaled high notes and
low notes on her way to fame.

Marilyn painted airplane parts in a Hollywood, California, factory, but she hoped to become a great actress. When a photographer snapped pictures of women helping with the war effort, her brilliant smile captivated the camera.

Goodbye, factory job.

Hello, studio contract!

Movie after movie, knowing just when to laugh or cry on cue,
Marilyn inched closer to stardom.

For years, Ella's velvety *shube-doobie-doos* wowed audiences. Jazz greats like Dizzy Gillespie, Louis Armstrong, and Duke Ellington couldn't wait to share the stage with her. She sold out her concert tours abroad.

But still, in her own country, too many doors were closed to her. In 1954, some club owners worried their customers wouldn't come if they played jazz music. Many wouldn't hire Black performers, and others would only showcase glamorous female stars like Lena Horne, Dinah Shore, and Edith Piaf. But Ella refused to give up on her dream.

Marilyn struggled with not having
her voice heard in a different way.
She dazzled fans with her baby blue
eyes and breathy *boo-boo-be-doos*. But
when she asked for better scripts
and a higher salary, the studio bosses
ignored her. As a woman working in
an industry run by men, she found
that her needs and her opinions
didn't matter to them.

Marilyn Monroe

Marilyn Monroe

One day, her manager handed her a new script—with a big singing role. He told her to listen to the best female singers so she could learn tempo and tone. Marilyn knew who the best was: her idol, Ella Fitzgerald!

Marilyn ran right out and bought a pile of Ella's records.

Over and over, she listened to Ella

vocalize,

harmonize,

and croon those jazzy blues as only she could.

Wrapping herself in Ella's voice, Marilyn understood how Ella's music was more than just notes that were sung. It was something special that came from deep inside of her. It reminded Marilyn of how she always put a little bit of herself into each character she portrayed onscreen.

Finally, the movie premiered. Critics praised Marilyn's performance. They loved her singing style and unique voice. Fans waited in long lines at the theater. The studio made lots of money.

Now when Marilyn spoke, her bosses paid attention. And reporters and photographers followed her everywhere.

GENTLEMEN PREFER BLONDES
MARILYN MONROE

Determined to thank Ella in person,
Marilyn bought a ticket to Ella's next show.

Ella took the stage.
She looked out at the audience.
Was that her favorite actress
sitting right there?

When the show was over
and the crowd thinned out,
only two women were left.

Sitting shoulder to shoulder, Ella and Marilyn chatted.
Marilyn idolized Ella because the singer always remained
true to herself. Not only did she love Ella for her voice,
but she also loved her as a person. Marilyn told Ella
how much she had learned by listening to her records.
Ella's heart sang, and in doing so, she had helped Marilyn
find her voice.

Ella was already famous for her voice. But, because of discrimination, not everyone was able to hear it. She told Marilyn that the owner of Hollywood's top nightspot, the Mocambo, refused to hire her.

Marilyn empathized with Ella. Although she didn't know what it was like to be singled out because of her race, she did know how it felt to be held back because she was a woman. As Ella helped Marilyn find her voice, now Marilyn wanted to do the same for her.

Putting their heads together, Marilyn and Ella hatched a plan.

Ella picked out her music,
practiced her songs, and polished
her vocals while Marilyn called the
owner of the club Mocambo to
make a deal with him.

She'd bring the media to the club's doorstep if
he'd hire Ella to perform. Reporters would write about it and
everyone would want to buy a ticket to Ella's shows there.
The owner said, "YES!"

On opening night, the club was packed. Ladies in sequined gowns.
Men in shiny tuxedos. Reporters and photographers crowded inside.

Draped in furs, Marilyn sat at a table up front, ready to cheer on her friend.

Head held high, Ella took center stage,
ready to wow the audience.

The band played.

Marilyn swayed to the melody.

Ella swayed to the rhythm.

Marilyn held her breath.

Ella filled her lungs . . .

and unleashed her musical
genius. She sang her heart
out for every man, woman,
and child whose voice
needed to be heard.

For the rest of their lives, Ella
Fitzgerald and Marilyn Monroe
remained good friends. Ella never
missed one of Marilyn's movies.
And Marilyn never stopped listening
to Ella's songs.

On the outside, these two stars
couldn't have looked more different.
But on the inside, they both understood
that sometimes even stars
need a little help to shine.

Ella and Marilyn may have had entirely different appearances, but they had a lot in common. Both had difficult childhoods, both struggled all their lives with shyness, and both had big dreams.

As a teenager, Ella had no real home. She lived on the streets and spent her time hanging around the Harlem Opera House and the Apollo Theater, watching the dancers, singers, and comedy acts. She won an Amateur Night competition and met bandleader Chick Webb. When he first saw her, he didn't want to hire her because she wore ragged clothes and her hair was a mess, but he was dazzled by her voice. She'd soon sing with Dizzy Gillespie, among many other greats, and became known as the Queen of Jazz, Lady Ella, and the First Lady of Song, but she remained a shy, retiring person when she wasn't immersed in her music. She gave credit to Marilyn when her career skyrocketed after the Mocambo club engagement. "I owe Marilyn Monroe a real debt," Ella said. "After that, I never had to play a small jazz club again." Ella saw past Marilyn's stunning looks and appreciated her intelligence and her compassion. "Marilyn was an unusual woman," Ella said. "A little ahead of her times."

As a child, Marilyn lived in nine foster homes, attended six elementary schools, and spent time in an orphanage. She stuttered when she was nervous, and was often quiet around adults. But she had a vivid imagination and loved telling stories to other children. She never complained about going to sleep because she would stand on her bed and act out movie scenes. When she became famous, movie studios tried to project an image of her as someone with lots of beauty and no brains. But Marilyn was very intelligent. She read all the classic works of literature and wrote poetry. She had a passion for justice, called Abraham Lincoln her hero, and was a proponent of the Civil Rights Movement before many people had the courage to speak up about it. Marilyn even owned her own movie company at a time when many women didn't own anything. She took acting classes so she could be seen as a "real" actress, even though many professionals thought she was already a gifted performer. And she always had great respect for Ella. She listened to Ella's recordings constantly so that she could learn to sing better. And when she had trouble falling asleep, she used Ella's voice as a lullaby. "My very favorite person," Marilyn said, "and I love her as a person as well as a singer, is Ella Fitzgerald."

As they worked hard to build their careers, both Ella and Marilyn struggled with discrimination. By the 1950s, they were already well-known.

But that didn't stop many venues from refusing to hire Ella. Perceived as having a plain face and being overweight, Ella didn't project the image of beauty that the club owners demanded from their performers. And even though Ella had a voice able to wow audiences all over the world, she still encountered discrimination because of the color of her skin, both onstage and off.

After getting off a plane in Hawaii on her way to her 1954 concert tour of Australia, Ella and her friends were not allowed to reboard, even to retrieve their belongings, and had to wait three days to arrange alternate transportation. Ella sued the airline, and won! Traveling through Jim Crow states was especially difficult because segregation was still the law of the land and officials didn't like that her manager insisted she perform only for integrated audiences. In 1955 at the Houston Music Hall, police barged into her dressing room and arrested Ella and her group. Released in time to perform their second show at the Music Hall, Ella said the police had the nerve to ask her for an autograph after she posted bond.

Marilyn was judged by her appearance also; the studio bosses called her straw-head. They thought she was too pretty to be smart, and they refused to give her any serious roles to play. By listening to Ella's records, Marilyn improved her own vocal abilities, and the movie with the big singing role, *Gentlemen Prefer Blondes*, was a smash hit. Marilyn was then able to leverage her star status to gain more control over her own career. The studio renegotiated her contract and finally gave her script and director approval. Marilyn was extremely grateful to Ella. So, when Marilyn found out that Ella was a victim of racial discrimination, she immediately had to stand up with Ella and do something about it. And they did. Together.

Ella Fitzgerald and Marilyn Monroe
Hollywood, California, 1954

PRIMARY SOURCES

"The Childhood Years – As Told By Marilyn Monroe." YouTube video, 9:32. "Marilyn Monroe Video Archives," July 3, 2015. https://www.youtube.com/watch?v=p34nlBUTyFM.

"Ella Fitzgerald – A Biography Part 1." YouTube video, 15:03. "ChristopherSyn1," February 19, 2014. https://www.youtube.com/watch?v=DhnJrSM3MHk.

"Marilyn Monroe being filmed by Joe Dimaggio – Frank Sinatra, Ella Fitzgerald and Sammy Davis Jr." YouTube video, 1:51. "Marilyn Monroe Video Archives," January 15, 2016. https://www.youtube.com/watch?v=HKHrP9fFNSo.

"Marilyn Monroe: Beyond The Legend (Hollywood Biography)." YouTube video, 59:39. "The Hollywood Collection," February 23, 2016. https://www.youtube.com/watch?v=lIfuJioOeJk.

"Marilyn Monroe – 'Do I Feel Happy In Life?'" YouTube video, 3:06. "Marilyn Monroe Video Archives," September 21, 2011. https://www.youtube.com/watch?v=fgBEI_VPjuw.

"Marilyn Monroe – Ella Fitzgerald And Mocambo Club." YouTube video, 1:06. "Marilyn Monroe Video Archives," August, 27, 2012. https://www.youtube.com/watch?v=6WhOqGtm7Kg.

"Marilyn Monroe Rare Live Television Appearance – 'Person To Person' Interview 1955." YouTube video, 14:26. "Marilyn Monroe Video Archives," August, 16, 2013. https://www.youtube.com/watch?v=L05TYBXwU3A&t=8s.

Telephone interviews with Audrey P. Franklyn, Ella Fitzgerald's promoter for thirty-seven years. June 8 and June 10, 2016.

Secondary Sources

A, Alex. "When Marilyn Monroe Stood up for Civil Rights and Changed Ella Fitzgerald's Life with One Phone Call," *The Vintage News*, August 3, 2016. https://www.thevintage-news.com/2016/08/03/prirority-time-marilyn-monroe-stood-civil-rights-changed-ella-fitzgeralds-life-one-phone-call-2/2.

Banner, Lois. *Marilyn: The Passion and the Paradox*. New York: Bloomsbury USA, 2012.

Brown, Peter Harry, and Patte B. Barnham. *Marilyn: The Last Take*. New York: Dutton, 1992.

Churchwell, Sarah. *The Many Lives of Marilyn Monroe*. New York: Metropolitan Books, 2005.

Darvell, Michael. *Marilyn and Ella*. London: 2008.

Encyclopedia of World Biography. "Ella Fitzgerald." *Encyclopedia.com*, June 7, 2019. https://www.encyclopedia.com/history/encyclopedias-almanacs-tran-scripts-and-maps/ella-fitzgerald.

Greer, Bonnie. *Marilyn and Ella Backstage at the Mocambo*. London: 2019.

Guiles, Fred Lawrence. *Norma Jean: The Life of Marilyn Monroe*. New York: McGraw-Hill Book Company, 1967.

Kliment, Bud, and Nathan Irvin Huggins. *Ella Fitzgerald*. Langhorne, Pennsylvania: Chelsea House Publishers, 1970.

Kniesedt, Kevin. "How Marilyn Monroe Changed Ella Fitzgerald's Life." *KNKX*, March 22, 2012. https://www.knkx.org/post/how-marilyn-monroe-changed-ella-fitzgeralds-life.

Loxton, Howard. "Marilyn and Ella." *British Theatre Guide*, June 5, 2016. https://www.brit-ishtheatreguide.info/reviews/marilynella-rev.

Monroe, Marilyn. *Fragments: Poems, Intimate Notes, Letters*, ed. Stanley Buchthal and Bernard Comment. New York: Farrar, Straus and Giroux, 2010.

Nicholson, Stuart. *Ella Fitzgerald: A Biography of the First Lady of Jazz*. New York: Charles Scribner's Sons, 1994.

Pinkney, Andrea Davis, and Brian Pinkney. *Ella Fitzgerald: The Tale of a Vocal Virtuosa*. New York: Jump at the Sun, 2007.

Rose, Jacqueline. "A Rumbling of Things Unknown," April 26, 2012, in the *London Review of Books* podcast, 57:56, https://www.lrb.co.uk/v34/n08/jacqueline-rose/a-rumbling-of-things-unknown.

Slatzer, Robert F. *The Marilyn Files*. New York: S.P.I. Books, 1992.

Steinem, Gloria. *Marilyn*. New York: Henry Holt & Company, 1988.

Talley, Heather Laine. "The Ugly Side of Lookism and What We Can Do About It." *HuffPost*, January 22, 2016. https://www.huffpost.com/entry/the-ugly-side-of-lookism_b_9042114.